THE HORROR OF THE BUBONIC PLAGUE

by Claire Throp

Consultant: Philip Parker
Author and historian

capstone

Infosearch books are published by Capstone Press,
1710 Roe Crest Drive, North Mankato, Minnesota 56003
www.mycapstone.com

Library of Congress Cataloging-in-Publication Data
Library of Congress Cataloging-in-Publication data is available on the Library of Congress website.

978-1-4846-4167-5 (library binding)
978-1-4846-4171-2 (paperback)
978-1-4846-4175-0 (eBook PDF)

Editorial Credits
Editor: Claire Throp
Designer: Clare Nicholas
Production Specialist: Kathy McColley
Media Researchers: Claire Throp and Izzi Howell
Illustrators: Ron Dixon and Clare Nicholas

Photo Credits
Alamy: Chronicle, 38, David Lyons, 26, GL Archive, 21, Granger Historical Picture Archive, 20, Josse Christophel, 10, Niday Picture Library, 25, Photo Researchers, Inc, 17, Pictorial Press Ltd, 23, Steve Taylor ARPS, 27, World History Archive, 16; Getty: MOLA, 12; iStock: duncan1890, 19, 29, ZU_09, 32; Shutterstock: Aksenenko Olga, 3, 44 -45 (dirt), ananaline, 41 (circle), blackboard1965, 15, Cosmin Manci, 43, Everett-Art, 33, eveleen, 5 (human outline), Everett Historical, 4, Ian Woolcock, 11, ktsdesign, 5, 41 (bacteria), Martial Red, 6 (skull and crossbones), Michal Szymanski, 7, Pakhnyushchy, 3, 37, 44, 45 (rat), RedKoala, 13 (gravestone), Roberto Castillo, 9, ShDmFch, 42, Sudowoodo, 13 (skull and crossbones on gravestone), Volodymyr Burdiak, 14; Superstock: Iberfoto/Iberfoto, cover; Wellcome Library, London: 1, 22, 24, 28, 31, 35, Kaufmann/Fabry, 39, Science Museum, London, Wellcome Images, 34.

Title page image is of a plague doctor from the 1600s.

Printed in the United States of America.
010365F17

Table of Contents

What Is Bubonic Plague?

Bubonic plague is one of history's deadliest killers. Millions of people have died. It is an often fatal disease that spreads quickly.

Bubonic plague is an **infection** of the **lymph nodes**. These are parts of the body that are meant to help protect against disease. **Symptoms** include large swellings called **buboes**. These can appear on the neck, armpits, and inner thighs. Sufferers can have fevers, headaches, chills, and feel tired and weak. Black patches may appear on the skin.

■ People infected with plague suffered from a number of symptoms, including buboes.

TYPES OF PLAGUE

There are three types of plague. A **bacterium** called *Yersinia pestis* is what causes it. The bacteria live in **rodents**, such as rats. Fleas feed on the blood of infected rats. When the rats die, the fleas might move on to humans. Any human bitten by an infected flea will also become infected. This is how bubonic plague spreads. Pneumonic plague is an infection of the lungs. This form is deadlier. It can spread when infected people cough or sneeze. The third type is septicemic plague, which is an infection of the blood. This can be from flea bites or contact with infected people or animals if the skin is cut or cracked.

■ Few people survived the plague before modern medicine became available. This chart shows the likelihood of death for a plague sufferer in the 1300s.

PLAGUE DEATH RATES

50% to 75%	90%	100%
Bubonic plague	Pneumonic plague	Septicemic plague

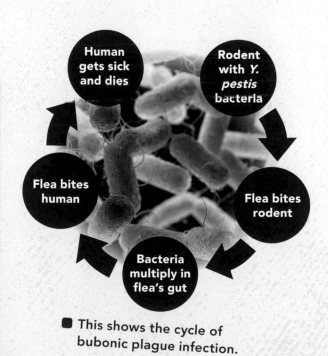

Human gets sick and dies

Rodent with *Y. pestis* bacteria

Flea bites human

Flea bites rodent

Bacteria multiply in flea's gut

■ This shows the cycle of bubonic plague infection.

What Was the Plague of Justinian?

By CE 395, the Roman Empire had become so large that it was split in two. The Western Empire was ruled from Rome. The Eastern Empire had its base in Constantinople (now Istanbul, Turkey). The first **pandemic** of bubonic plague in Europe affected the eastern Roman Empire. A pandemic affects millions of people over many countries. The Empire was ruled by Justinian I. The plague of CE 541–542 became known as the Plague of Justinian.

PROCOPIUS OF CAESAREA

Symptoms of the Plague of Justinian were described by Procopius of Caesarea, a historian from that time. His report of the plague mentioned fever and that "a bubonic swelling developed" on parts of the body.

FATAL FACTS

Procopius suggested that the plague at its peak killed up to 10,000 people a day.

Procopius said the plague actually began in Egypt, although today it is thought it began in Asia. Ships and the rats traveling on them brought the disease to the Roman Empire.

After Constantinople, it spread across Europe as far as Ireland. It also hit Africa, the Middle East, and Asia in the next few years. It is thought that between 30 and 50 million people died during this first pandemic. The pandemic did not end until the mid-700s.

EFFECTS

The bubonic plague had a major effect on the Roman Empire. Justinian had been battling to retake land captured by **barbarians**. But soon there were not enough soldiers left to fight. Many died. Fewer people were alive to pay taxes, so the emperor also had less money to pay soldiers. As a result, Justinian was unable to bring the two parts of the Empire together again. It is thought that the weakening of the Empire is one of the reasons that led to Muslims defeating it in the 600s.

■ Emperor Justinian I caught the plague, but he survived.

What Was the Black Death?

The plague first appeared in China in the 1330s. It became known as the Black Death because of the black patches that appeared on the skin. It swept across Asia, then Europe and finally Russia. It is thought that it followed the main **trade** routes. The Black Death is said to have killed 50 million people in about four years. About half of these deaths were in Asia and Africa. The other half were in Europe, where between a quarter and a half of the **population** died.

■ This map shows how the Black Death spread.

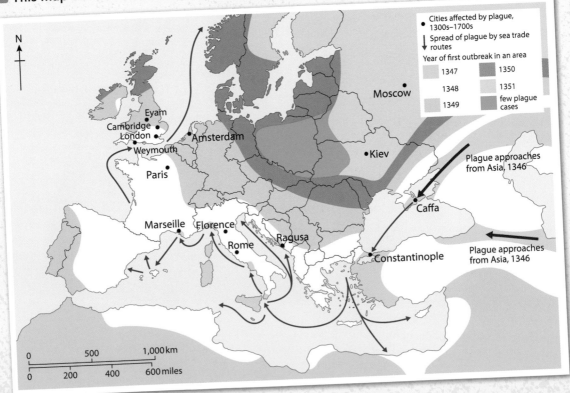

Cities affected by plague, 1300s–1700s

Spread of plague by sea trade routes

Year of first outbreak in an area

1347	1350
1348	1351
1349	few plague cases

N

Moscow

Eyam
Cambridge
London
Amsterdam
Weymouth
Kiev
Paris

Plague approaches from Asia, 1346

Marseille Florence
Rome Ragusa
Caffa
Constantinople

Plague approaches from Asia, 1346

0   500   1,000 km
0   200   400   600 miles

CAFFA

Italian Gabriele de' Mussi wrote about the Black Death in the late 1300s. The city of Caffa (now Feodosija, Ukraine) was under siege by the Mongol army. The Mongols threw plague-infected bodies over the city walls. Many of the people who lived there caught the disease. Survivors who fled the city helped to spread the plague to Europe.

ITALY

The "Black Vomit," as it was known, appeared in Italy in winter 1347. By spring 1348, it had moved northward to Florence. Florence was already suffering from a failed crop, which led to there being less food available. This meant people were weaker and less able to fight off disease. Doctors charged a lot of money to see a patient. Many people died of starvation because they couldn't afford to eat after seeing a doctor. It is thought that 45–75 percent of the city died in six months.

■ Doctors could do little for people who caught the Black Death.

COUNCIL OF EIGHT

A council of eight of the wisest men in Florence was set up to sort out the city. But there was not a lot they could do. They did make sure that dead bodies were taken outside the city walls. This was thought to limit the spread of the plague.

Giovanni Boccaccio

Giovanni Boccaccio was an Italian writer. He wrote about the plague in Florence. He is best known for his book *The Decameron* (1353). Boccaccio described how **quacks** took advantage of sick people. Quacks sold medicine that they knew would not work.

This is a page from Boccaccio's *The Decameron*.

BRITAIN

The first sign of the Black Death in Britain was at the port of Melcombe Regis in Dorset in June 1348. Ports are places where many ships come to load and unload goods. As the plague was spread along trade routes, ports were places where plague could easily enter a country.

Weymouth (shown here) and Melcombe Regis were separate ports in the mid-1300s. They became the single port of Weymouth in 1571.

HISTORY UNLOCKED

A writer who lived at the time, Geoffrey the Baker, wrote of the plague's arrival in Britain. It first began "in the towns and ports joining on the seacoasts." It killed so many people "that there were almost none left alive."

The plague spread to Wales, Ireland, and the north of England in 1349. At this time, Scotland invaded Durham in northern England. They decided to take advantage of the city's weakness. It backfired, though. People in Scotland began to die of the plague in 1350.

LONDON

The plague hit London in September 1348. It soon became impossible to bury those who had died in the way the dead were normally buried. There wasn't room. So plague pits were dug. These were mass burial sites where bodies were piled on top of each other. Sometimes, they were piled up to five bodies deep. Children were usually placed in the spaces between adults.

This mass grave in London was dug for the many people who died of the Black Death.

FATAL FACTS

It is thought that half of London's population – about 40,000 people – died during the Black Death.

HISTORY UNLOCKED

A 14th-century book from the cathedral of Rochester, England, included a description of the Black Death.

"Men and women carried the bodies of their own little ones to church on their shoulders and threw them into mass graves, from which arose such a stink that it was barely possible for anyone to go past a churchyard."

RUSSIA

The plague continued to spread. It reached Russia in 1351–1352. One way the Russians tried to stop plague was to build a church to a saint. Many new churches were built in very short period of time, particularly in Novgorod where plague hit hardest. Russians blamed witches for the plague. In Pskov, in the late 1300s, 12 women were burned alive. They were thought to be witches and responsible for a plague **outbreak**. Their deaths did not stop further outbreaks from happening, however.

■ Many European cities lost a large percentage of their population during 1347–1351. This graph shows just a few of those cities.

PERCENTAGE OF THE POPULATION WHO DIED FROM PLAGUE

60% to 70% — Hamburg, Germany

45% to 75% — Florence, Italy

35% — Dublin, Ireland

50% — Paris, France

50% — London, England

How Did Doctors Deal with the Black Death?

Medical knowledge was poor at the time of the Black Death. Doctors did not understand how disease spread. Bacteria and germs were not discovered by scientists until the mid-1600s and the mid-1800s. Doctors thought that bad smells—called miasma—were responsible for disease. They wore masks with long beaks full of herbs to try to protect them from miasma.

One of the early "cures" for plague was to strap a live chicken to a bubo.

In 1299, Pope Boniface VIII was the leader of the Catholic Church, which was very powerful in Europe. He banned doctors from investigating the bodies of dead people. This meant that it was difficult to discover more about how the human body worked.

HIPPOCRATES AND GALEN

So doctors continued to follow the work of Greek doctors Hippocrates (460–370 BC) and Galen (AD 130–216). They believed that illness was a result of the "Four Humors" in the body being out of balance. The humors were liquids found in the body, and Galen believed that blood was the most important. Bloodletting involved releasing blood from a person's body by various methods. It was carried out by doctors as a cure for many health issues, not just plague. But it probably did nothing more than make the person weaker.

In the 1500s and 1600s, doctors learned more about the body and were able to disprove many of the earlier ideas. However, the belief that the humors of the body were linked with a person's health lasted until after 1700.

Hippocrates is known as the "father of medicine."

HISTORY UNLOCKED

Many people thought that illness was a punishment from God. Hippocrates believed it had natural causes.

"Sickness is not sent by the gods or taken away by them. It has a natural basis. If we can find the cause, we can find the cure."

CAUSES OF THE PLAGUE

Lack of medical knowledge about the plague meant that people had to come up with their own ideas. Some people thought it was to do with the movement of the planets. Others believed it was punishment from God. Flagellants thought that punishing themselves would encourage God to take away the plague. Some blamed groups who were seen as "different," such as Jewish people. Many thought that bad air was the problem. People would hold sponges soaked in vinegar close to their noses to avoid catching the plague. It didn't work!

■ In the Netherlands, people known as flagellants whipped themselves in the streets.

QUARANTINE

One of the early **public health** measures for stopping plague was **quarantine**. Ships carrying goods for trade were not allowed to land until they could prove everyone was healthy and the goods had been **disinfected**. This did help to contain the plague in some cases.

Quarantine also involved keeping infected people away from healthy people in order to keep the disease from spreading. In 1377, Ragusa (now Dubrovnik, Croatia) was the first city to use quarantine. Visitors from plague-infected areas had to be kept away from healthy people for 30 days. Other cities in France and Italy carried out similar measures, but increased the length of time to 40 days. The word "quarantine" comes from the Italian words for 40 days: *quaranta giorni*.

■ Doctors burst buboes to try to cure the plague.

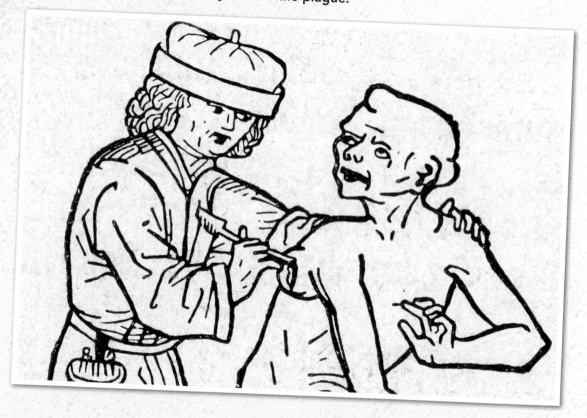

Quarantine rules were not always followed. Sometimes, officials did not set up quarantine measures quickly enough. At other times, people worried that their livelihoods would be affected if others thought their town was affected by plague. Who would want to travel to or buy goods from a plague town?

What Was the Effect of the Black Death?

A system of power had been in place in Europe for many years. Usually a king or queen ruled a country. Noblemen and knights held a lot of the land. **Peasants** were given, or rented, a small amount of land, but they had to work on the land owned by the knights in return.

FEWER WORKERS

After the Black Death, there were fewer people to do the work. This meant that people who survived were able to ask for more money and better working conditions. This pushed up wages until the English Parliament passed a law to limit the rise in wages. Peasants were angry about this. The Peasants' Revolt took place in England in 1381. There were other revolts throughout Europe. The system of power—sometimes known as the feudal system—broke down.

In some countries, plague led to a shortage of food. Crops were left in fields because there were not enough people to harvest them. This meant less food for people to eat. Some starved to death.

The number of people who died from plague caused survivors to think about life differently. Religious beliefs changed for some people. They saw that religion didn't help protect against disease.

King Richard II met with the peasants during the Peasants' Revolt of 1381.

JEWISH PEOPLE

Jewish people had been treated badly before throughout Europe, but it got worse. Fewer Jewish people seemed to be affected by plague. Some people now think this was because of their better **hygiene**. At the time, people wrongly thought that Jewish people were poisoning the water. Many Jewish people were forced to leave their homes to escape the harsh treatment they faced as a result of other people's fear and anger.

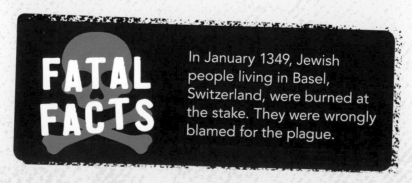

FATAL FACTS

In January 1349, Jewish people living in Basel, Switzerland, were burned at the stake. They were wrongly blamed for the plague.

What Was the Great Plague?

Outbreaks of bubonic plague had appeared in Britain every 20 or 30 years since 1348. But the Great Plague of 1665 was the worst. The plague first appeared in the spring in one of the poorer areas of London: St. Giles-in-the-Fields. By the end of May 1665, 43 people had died. September saw the greatest number of deaths in one week: 7,165. It is believed that 15 percent of London's population died of plague in 1665.

■ Bills of mortality were printed each week to show the number of people who had died.

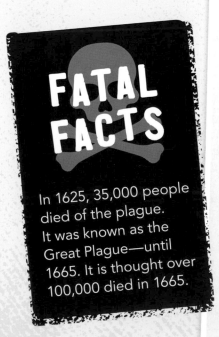

FATAL FACTS

In 1625, 35,000 people died of the plague. It was known as the Great Plague—until 1665. It is thought over 100,000 died in 1665.

The Diseases and Casualties this Week.

Abortive	4	Imposthume	8
Aged	45	Infants	22
Breeding	1	Kingfevil	4
Broken legge	1	Lethargy	1
Broke her fcull by a fall in the ftreet at St. Mary VVoolchurch	1	Livergrown	1
		Meagrome	1
		Palfie	1
Childbed	28	Plague	4237
Chrifomes	9	Purples	2
Confumption	126	Quinfie	5
Convulfion	89	Rickets	23
Cough	1	Rifing of the Lights	18
Dropfie	53	Rupture	1
Feaver	348	Scurvy	1
Flox and Small-pox	11	Shingles	3
Flux	1	Spotted Feaver	166
Frighted	2	Stilborn	4
Gowt	1	Stone	2
Grief	3	Stopping of the ftomach	17
Griping in the Guts	79	Strangury	3
Head-mould-fhot	1	Suddenly	2
Jaundies	7	Surfeit	74
		Teeth	111
		Thrush	6
		Tiffick	9
		Ulcer	1
		Vomiting	10
		Winde	4
		Wormes	20

Christned	Males	90	Buried	Males	2777	Plague—4237
	Females	81		Females	2791	
	In all	171		In all	5568	

Increased in the Burials this Week ———— 249
Parishes clear of the Plague —— 27 Parishes Infected —— 103

The Affize of Bread fet forth by Order of the Lord Maior and Court of Aldermen, A penny Wheaten Loaf to contain Nine Ounces and a half, and three half-penny White Loaves the like weight.

LOCKED IN

When the plague hit London, people fled the city if they could. Poorer people had to stay. Plague **victims** were shut in their homes for 40 days and had a large red cross painted on the door. Watchmen patrolled the streets to make sure the houses stayed sealed. Often, this meant that any healthy people died when they might have survived. Sometimes they died of starvation—often, not enough food was provided by **charities**. If people were not locked up in their own homes, they were sent to pest houses. These were in remote areas and were an attempt to prevent the plague spreading. These measures did not seem to work.

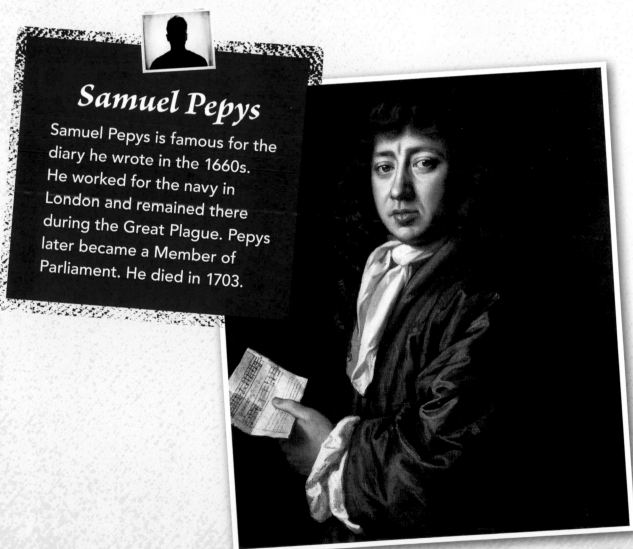

Samuel Pepys

Samuel Pepys is famous for the diary he wrote in the 1660s. He worked for the navy in London and remained there during the Great Plague. Pepys later became a Member of Parliament. He died in 1703.

NEW JOBS

Searchers of the dead had to check dead bodies to see if they had died of plague or something else. Searchers were often old women. People knew to avoid these women because they carried a white stick.

Another job was that of collecting the dead bodies. These men traveled by horse and cart. They would call out, "Bring out your dead" while ringing a bell. Bodies would be taken to one of the plague pits, where they were buried in mass graves.

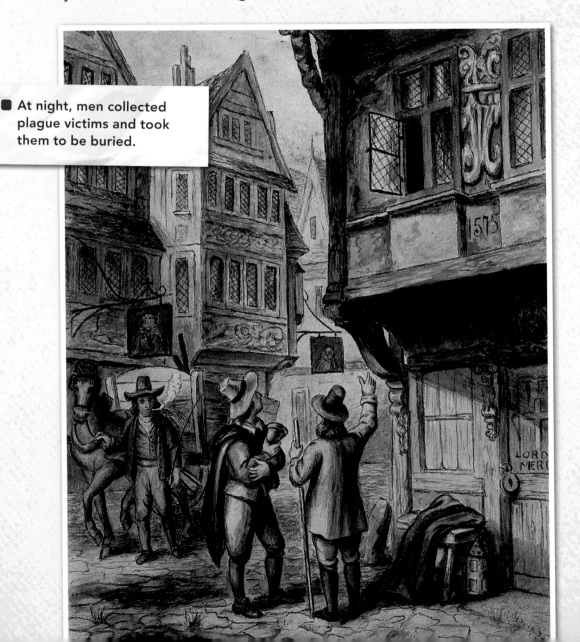

At night, men collected plague victims and took them to be buried.

NO IMPROVEMENT

Understanding of the causes of plague and how to deal with it had not improved much since the mid-1300s. One of the first things done in London possibly made things worse. It was believed that cats and dogs spread the plague. Samuel Pepys claimed that 40,000 dogs and about 200,000 cats were killed. Those cats would probably have killed a lot of the rats.

Rats carrying the plague were attracted by all the garbage in the streets of cities. In those days, city streets were often dirty. There were no sewers—people just emptied their toilet waste out of a window and onto the street.

■ Large plague pits were dug to bury all the victims.

23

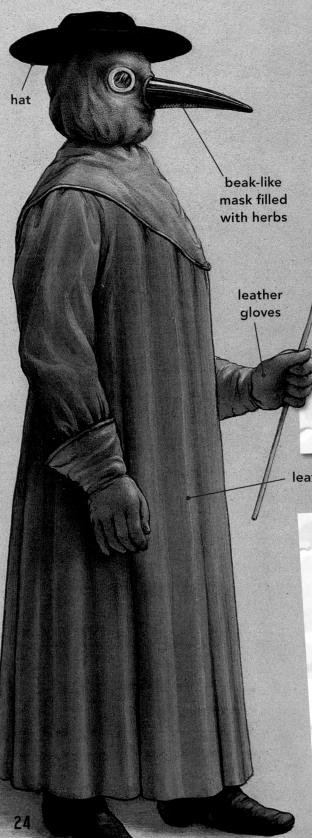

hat

beak-like
mask filled
with herbs

leather
gloves

leather cloak

PLAGUE CURES

At the time of the Great Plague, many doctors used a book written by a Dutch doctor named Ysbrand van Diemerbroeck. The book was called *Several Choice Histories of the Medicines, Manner and Method used in the Cure of the Plague*. Each chapter tells the story of a plague patient. It lists what measures were unsuccessful or successful in curing them. Advice for doctors is included at the end of each chapter.

■ Doctors wore strange outfits when visiting people who had plague.

HISTORY UNLOCKED

As soon as the plague returned, quacks appeared. They said they had the pills and powders that could help to prevent or even cure the plague. One advert gave these instructions to cure the plague:

"If anyone is infected, and finds themselves ill, then presently let them (without delay) take this powder, and then to bed and sweat carefully three hours."

Tobacco was thought to be good for people in the 1600s. People believed that smoking tobacco would keep the bad air out of their body. Others sniffed a sponge soaked in vinegar.

GOD'S PUNISHMENT

People still believed that the plague was a punishment from God. King Charles II announced rules for trying to prevent the plague. One encouraged people to go to public prayers on Wednesdays and Fridays. Collections of money were to be given to the poor so that God would remove the plague.

■ King Charles II left London to escape the plague.

LOST JOBS

Trade with plague towns was stopped. Scotland announced the **border** with England would be closed. Then trade with other countries was stopped. Many people lost their jobs as a result.

What Happened Outside London?

Many towns and villages traded with London. This allowed the plague to spread easily. Ports along the coasts provided another way in for the disease.

When they heard about plague in London, many towns started to use measures they had used before. They cleaned up the streets and were careful about the travelers they let into their town. However, sometimes that wasn't enough.

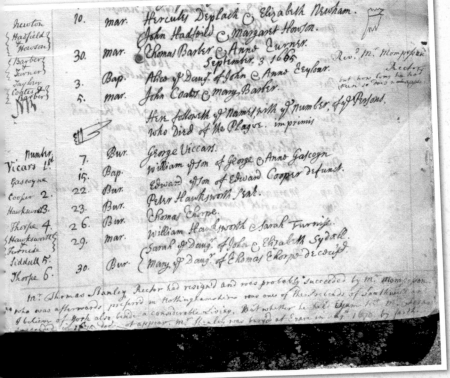

EYAM

In September 1665, a delivery of cloth from London caused plague to spread through the village of Eyam, Derbyshire. George Viccars opened the package of cloth. Infected fleas were also inside the package. Viccars was the first to die.

■ George Viccars is listed in the Eyam parish register as the first victim of plague.

Some villagers wanted to flee. But William Mompesson, leader of the church, persuaded them to stay. The villagers quarantined themselves on June 24, 1666. They did this even though they knew it would probably mean death for most of them. In August 1666, Elizabeth Hancock lost six of her children and her husband. She had to bury them herself because there was no one else left to do it. The last man to die of plague was Abraham Morten. Seventeen other members of the Morten family died of the plague too.

AN UNSELFISH ACT

Nobody knows exactly how many people lived in Eyam, but 260 out of at least 350 villagers died. Many lives in northern England were saved because of the villagers' unselfish act.

■ Money was placed in holes on the top of this stone in exchange for food during the plague.

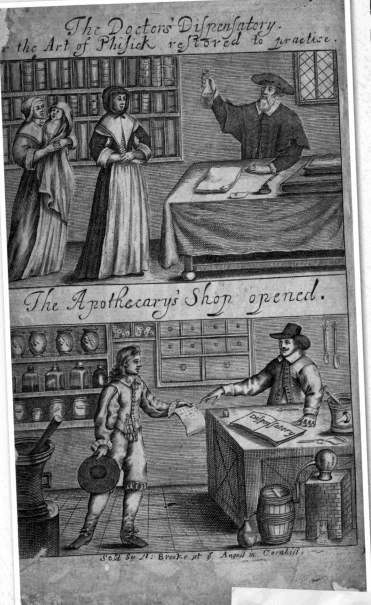

The Doctors' Dispensatory.
or the Art of Phisick restored to practise.

The Apothecary's Shop opened.

Sold by N: Brooke at ý Angell in Cornhill.

Apothecaries gave advice as well as medicine to patients.

CAMBRIDGE

In the village of St Clement's, Cambridge, 13-year-old Jacob King was the first to die. He fell ill on August 13, 1665. His father bought medicine from the local apothecary. It did not work, though. Buboes appeared in Jacob's armpits: it was definitely bubonic plague. On August 15, Jacob died. Soon there were many more deaths.

APOTHECARIES

Apothecaries prepared and sold medicine. Apothecaries were important at this time because they tended to stay behind in areas hit by plague. Some doctors fled, while others refused to deal with plague victims. Many doctors who did stay, died.

HISTORY UNLOCKED

Sir Edward Southcote from St Clement's was five at the time of the plague. He later wrote to his son about "people lying dead in the highway that nobody dared bury."

CROPS

By mid-August, corn was ready to be harvested. But there were too few laborers left to do the work. Farmers were desperate for help. They had to pay more to get workers from outside Cambridge.

LONGER TO RECOVER

About 12 percent of the population of Cambridge died—920 people. This may not seem much compared to the huge number of deaths in London. But smaller towns and villages took much longer to recover from that many deaths. Numbers of marriages and of children being born in Cambridge did not reach the levels found before the plague again till the late 1670s.

■ In 1665, a law stated that every parish had to build a pest house. This pest house and plague pit were in London. Cambridge had groups of these wooden huts in fields.

Where Else Did the Plague Appear?

Outbreaks of plague occurred regularly, not just in Britain but across Europe and Russia. Some outbreaks killed only a small number of people. Others caused a lot more damage.

■ Marseille was badly affected by the plague in 1720.

FRANCE

The last major outbreak in Europe was in Marseille, France, in 1720. Half the city's population—50,000 people—died. Quarantines had been used for many years in Europe. A ship that had carried victims of plague was banned from unloading in Marseille. But it is thought that some people managed to offer enough money to be allowed to leave the ship. Soon, the plague spread. Toulon and poorer areas of Marseille were badly affected. By September 1720, bodies were piled in the streets.

News of the Marseille outbreak reached the rest of Europe. Writer Daniel Defoe wrote a book called *A Journal of the Plague Year* after hearing about it. His story is based on the plague of 1665.

CHEVALIER ROZE

One of the heroes of this time was Chevalier Nicolas Roze, a French nobleman. He helped to bring order to the streets. He gathered 100 prisoners and 40 other people to hand out food and other supplies. They also removed dead bodies. Roze even got off his horse and lifted rotting bodies onto his shoulders. He wanted to show that if he could do it, so could the others. Only five of this group of people, including Roze himself, survived.

STRICTER QUARANTINE

After the Marseille disaster, quarantine rules became even stricter. Many city rulers tried to limit trade. They thought this would help to prevent more outbreaks.

Trade routes included the Silk Road, which began in China.

RUSSIA

Russia's last major plague outbreak took place in 1770–1772. Kiev was the first city to report deaths from plague in September 1770. Victims were shut up in their homes; their belongings were burned. By the end of the year, 4,000 people had died.

Officials in Moscow, however, did not want to admit that there was another major outbreak. So they continued trading with other European cities. The plague probably came into Moscow from infected wool or silk. It spread quickly through cloth manufacturing areas of the city. A riot against the plague took place in September 1771. Catherine the Great, Russia's leader, set up a commission to look into prevention of the plague. This improved quarantine measures and brought an end to burning people's belongings.

■ Empress Catherine the Great ordered that plague prevention be improved.

DEADLY PLAGUE

It is thought that about 200,000 died in Moscow, which made it deadlier than the Great Plague of London in 1665. This was partly because there were not as many rich people in Moscow who could afford to leave. The fact that the government had not told people about the plague probably didn't help. Doctors worked hard to deal with the plague. But their work was never going to be enough because they still thought miasma was the cause of it. After the plague in Moscow, there was an increase in the number of people becoming doctors and of hospitals being built.

What Was the Modern Plague?

The third plague pandemic started in an area of China called Yunnan in 1855. It had spread to Hong Kong by 1894. It moved on to India, Africa, Australia, and the United States. This pandemic is thought to have caused 10–15 million deaths, mostly in India.

HISTORY UNLOCKED

Plague medals were given to people who helped during the Hong Kong plague outbreak. These included nurses and soldiers.

This was the last plague pandemic. Chinese scientists noted that many rats died in the months before the plague reached the human population. Soon a link was made: rats were involved in causing plague.

INDIA

Plague reached India in 1896. At first, only ports such as Bombay were affected. But by 1899, it had spread inland. Western and northern India were the worst affected areas.

The British ruled India at the time. British doctors claimed that the disease was one of "filth." Their quarantine measures were thought to be extremely harsh on local people. After the Indians rioted, the British were forced to back down. They also realized it would be impossible to quarantine all the plague-affected areas.

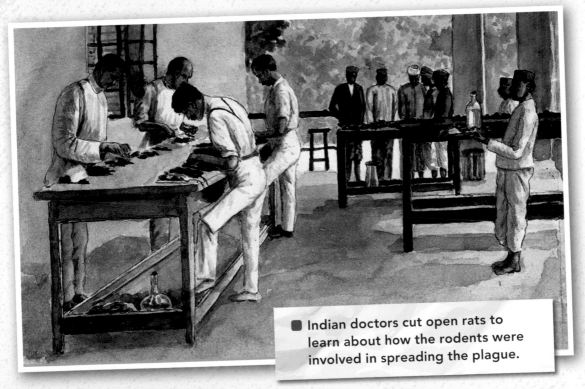

■ Indian doctors cut open rats to learn about how the rodents were involved in spreading the plague.

THE PLAGUE SPREADS

The first appearance of plague in the mainland United States was in early 1900. It was probably due to rats entering the country on ships from Asia. San Francisco, California, had an area known as Chinatown. Many Chinese people lived there in poor conditions. It was Chinatown that saw the first victims. A medical expert, Joseph J. Kinyoun, announced the deaths were from bubonic plague.

GAGE'S DENIAL

In June 1900, California was quarantined. Governor Henry Gage managed to get the quarantine lifted, but his reasons were not for the good of the people. Gage claimed the plague did not exist. He did not want California to lose out on trade due to quarantine. He strongly criticized Kinyoun. But the plague began to kill more people and leave others fearing for their lives. Gage's actions may have resulted in more deaths than were necessary. Kinyoun was later proved correct—there were 113 deaths from bubonic plague.

The last outbreak in a major US city was in 1924–1925 in Los Angeles. Since then, only small numbers of plague cases have been known in the western United States.

■ This map shows plague outbreaks in the 1800s and early 1900s.

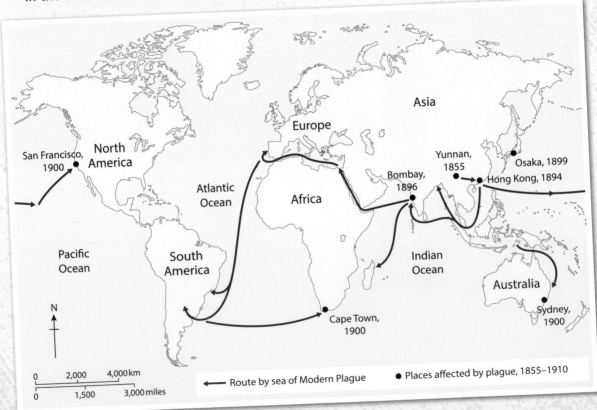

AUSTRALIA

Australia suffered 12 outbreaks of bubonic plague between 1900 and 1925. Many doctors still thought of the plague as one that was spread person to person. But public health officials knew that rats were now thought to be the problem. They set about trying to prevent the entry of plague into their country by catching as many rats as possible. However, in January 1900, Arthur Paine was the first plague victim in Sydney. A public health department was set up. Some of the doctors working there went on to greatly improve ways of dealing with the plague in the following years.

FATAL FACTS

There were 1,371 plague cases in Australia and 535 deaths.

NO FOURTH PANDEMIC

Over the next 50 years, there were further outbreaks. But in many countries, these were on a smaller scale. People who caught the disease could now be treated. This is probably why there has not been a fourth pandemic.

How Was Bubonic Plague Finally Controlled?

It took many hundreds of years, but finally scientists discovered how bubonic plague spread. They found that rodents and fleas were responsible. By the mid-1800s, knowledge of disease and illness had improved. In 1864, French scientist Louis Pasteur had shown that germs cause disease. Robert Koch, a German scientist, had investigated how different bacteria cause different diseases.

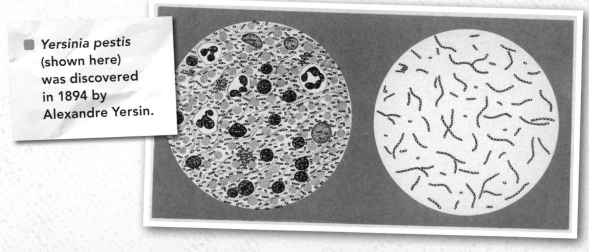

Yersinia pestis (shown here) was discovered in 1894 by Alexandre Yersin.

YERSINIA PESTIS

French scientist Alexandre Yersin was sent to Hong Kong when the plague broke out there in 1894. He took samples from buboes and investigated them. He discovered that the cause of bubonic plague was a bacterium. A Japanese scientist, Kitasato Shibasaburo, also found the bacterium. But it was eventually named after Yersin: *Yersinia pestis*.

Alexandre Yersin

Alexandre Yersin was born in Switzerland in 1863. After moving to France, Yersin trained in science. He then worked as a doctor on steamships. In 1892, he joined the Colonial Health Service and made his name discovering the cause of bubonic plague. Yersin lived in Vietnam for many years, until his death in 1943.

YERSIN

FLEAS

In Karachi, Pakistan, in 1898, French scientist Paul-Louis Simond discovered that fleas carried the plague between brown rats. Those fleas spread the plague to people when there are no longer enough live rats to bite.

UNDER CONTROL

Once these breakthroughs had been made, plague was easier to control. Chemicals called **insecticides** could be used to reduce the number of fleas. The introduction of **antibiotics** helped to lower the death rate. Nowadays, if given soon enough, antibiotics can mean that fewer than 15 percent of plague sufferers die.

Does the Bubonic Plague Still Exist?

Plague still exists today, but it is not as common. It does not kill anywhere near the number of people it once did. Between 1,000 and 2,000 cases are reported to the World Health Organisation (WHO) each year. However, scientists think that *Yersinia pestis* can be found in about 200 species of rodents around the world. This means it's possible that there could be another major plague outbreak in the future. It is also thought that plague can reappear in a place that has been free of it for many years. Algeria, for example, had a plague outbreak 57 years after the last one.

FATAL FACTS

Afghanistan had its first-ever plague outbreak in 2007. Seventeen people died after eating infected camel meat.

AFRICA

Most human cases since 1990 have been in Africa. From 2000 to 2009, the Democratic Republic of Congo had the largest number of plague cases in the world. War has probably been part of the reason for this. Health services at times of war can be less effective, particularly in remote areas.

Scientists think that plague may become more common in East Africa. More land is used for crops, which can lead to more rodents, as there is a reliable source of food.

LONG-LASTING BACTERIA

Researchers have discovered that *Yersinia pestis* can survive in soil for a very long time. Many rodents are animals that burrow underground. They may take in the bacteria and spread it to other rodents. It has also been found that there are some rodent species that seem to have developed a resistance to the plague bacteria. This means they can survive for longer with *Yersinia pestis* in their system. The longer they survive, the more chance of plague spreading.

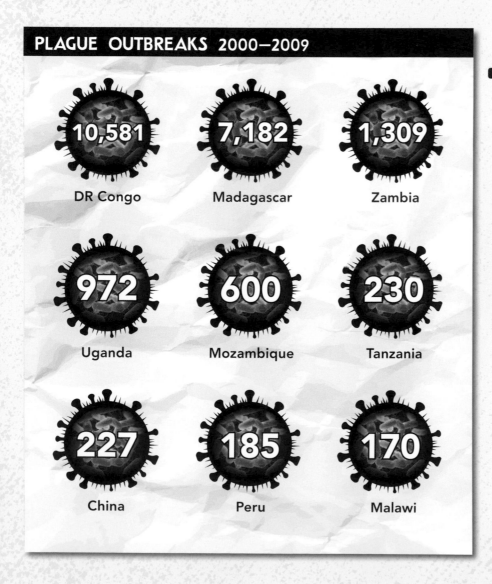

PLAGUE OUTBREAKS 2000–2009

10,581 DR Congo

7,182 Madagascar

1,309 Zambia

972 Uganda

600 Mozambique

230 Tanzania

227 China

185 Peru

170 Malawi

In the first 10 years of the 21st century, nearly 22,000 people were infected with plague. This chart shows the countries that were most affected.

LEARNING MORE

Ideas about the causes of the plague can change over time. Some people even think the Black Death was a mixture of different diseases, including anthrax, a cattle disease. Other scientists have suggested that gerbils, not rats, were the cause. They have looked at weather patterns in central Asia in the years before an outbreak. They think the weather was likely to have caused an increase in the number of gerbils in Asia. These would have been taken to Europe along trade routes.

■ **Were gerbils responsible for the Black Death?**

NEW INFORMATION

Scientists have been doing tests on skeletons from the AD 500s found in a burial site near Munich, Germany. In one of the teeth, they found *Yersinia pestis*, the same bacteria that caused the Black Death. This shows that the Plague of Justinian was caused by *Yersinia pestis* and that it spread further than originally thought.

FINDING OUT FASTER

Scientists have developed an easy, cheap, and fast way of finding out if someone has bubonic plague. A small rod called a dipstick that holds an **antibody** is dipped into an infected person's blood. If the plague bacterium is in the blood, it will show up. Plague can kill very quickly, so it is important to identify it as soon as possible. Normally blood must be sent to a laboratory to be tested. This can take a long time and even longer in remote areas. The new test will take a matter of minutes.

We will probably never know exactly how many people have died from bubonic plague over the years. But scientists are continuing to work hard to find new ways to fight it.

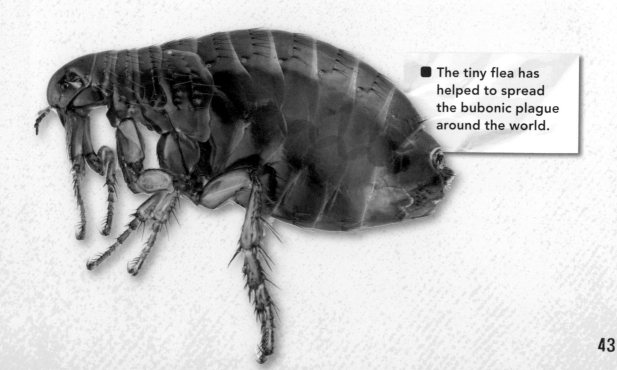

■ The tiny flea has helped to spread the bubonic plague around the world.

Timeline

541–542

1st pandemic: The Plague of Justinian affects Constantinople before spreading around the world.

1347–1351

2nd pandemic: The Black Death spreads through Europe.

1349–1353

Giovanni Boccaccio writes *The Decameron*.

1377

Quarantine is used for the first time in Ragusa (now Dubrovnik, Croatia).

1665–1666

The Great Plague kills thousands in Britain. Samuel Pepys describes the Great Plague in his diary.
The villagers of Eyam, Derbyshire, show great selflessness in quarantining themselves, saving many lives in the north of England.

1720

The last major plague outbreak in Europe happens in Marseille, France.

1722

A Journal of the Plague Year by Daniel Defoe is published.

1770–1772

The Great Plague in Russia kills thousands.

1855

3rd pandemic: The Modern Plague begins in China.

1894

French scientist Alexandre Yersin discovers that the cause of the bubonic plague is a bacterium. It is now called *Yersinia pestis*.

1896

The plague reaches India.

1898

French scientist Paul-Louis Simond shows that fleas carry the plague between rats and on to humans when the rats die.

1900

January
May

Arthur Paine is the first plague victim in Sydney, Australia. The first appearance of plague in the United States is found in San Francisco's Chinatown.

GLOSSARY

antibiotic (an-tee-by-ah-tik)—drug that kills bacteria and is used to cure infections and disease

antibody (AN-ti-bah-dee)—substance in a person's blood that destroys other substances that carry disease

bacterium (plural: bacteria) (bak-TEER-ee-um)—very small living things that exist all around you and inside you; some bacteria cause disease

barbarians people from countries outside the Roman Empire. The Romans thought they were uncivilized and violent.

border (BOR-der)—dividing line between two places

bubo (BYU-bo)—swelling on the body, often under the armpit or on the inner thigh

charity (CHAYR-uh-tee)—group that raises money or collects goods to help people in need

disinfect (dis-in-FEKT)—use chemicals to kill germs

hygiene (hye-JEEN)—level to which people keep themselves or their surroundings clean, especially to prevent disease

infection (in-FEK-shun)—disease in part of a person's body that is caused by germs or bacteria

insecticide (in-SEK-tuh-side)—chemical used to kill insects

lymph nodes (LYMF NODES)—small, bean-shaped glands that can be found in the neck, under the arms and on the inner thighs. They are part of the immune system, which helps to protect the body from disease.

outbreak (OWT-brayk)—when a number of people become ill at the same time from the same cause

pandemic (pan-DEM-ik)—when a disease spreads over a wide area and affects many people

peasant (PEZ-uhnt)—landless farmer who rents farmland from landowners

population (pop-yuh-LAY-shuhn)—people living in a place or country

public health (PUB-lik HELTH)—to do with the health of the whole population

quack (KWAK)—untrained person who claims to have knowledge or treatments that can prevent or cure diseases

quarantine (KWOR-uhn-teen)—keep a person, animal or plant away from others to stop a disease from spreading

rodent (ROHD-uhnt)—small mammal such as a rat, gerbil or squirrel

symptom (SIMP-tuhm)— sign that suggests a person is ill or has a health problem

trade (TRADE)—buying and selling of goods such as food and cloth

victim (VIK-tuhm)—person who suffers from a disease

READ MORE

Farndon, John. *Plague! The Sickening History of Medicine*. Minneapolis, Minn.: Hungry Tomato, 2017.

Jankowski Mahoney, Emily. *The Black Death: Bubonic Plague attacks Europe*. World History. Farmington Hills, Mich.: Lucent Press, 2017.

Jarrow, Gail. *Bubonic Panic: When Plague Invaded America*. Honesdale, Pa.: Calkins Creek, 2016.

Jeffrey, Gary. *The Black Death Graphic Medieval History*. St Catharines, ONT, Canada: Crabtree Publishing, 2014.

Oldfield, Pamela. *The Great Plague. My Story*. New York: Scholastic, 2008.

Internet Sites

FactHound offers a safe, fun way to find Internet sites related to this book. All of the sites on FactHound have been researched by our staff.

Here's all you do:

Visit *www.facthound.com*

Type in this code: 9781484641675

Critical Thinking Questions

Which parts of this book did you find the most interesting? What subjects would you like to know more about?

Do you think it was fair that healthy people were locked in their houses with members of their family who were suffering from plague?

Why do you think that most cases of plague now happen in Africa? Support your answer using information from at least two other texts or valid Internet sources.

INDEX